CALIFORNIA EDITION

REAL ESTATE

How to Profit from ADU's

To Creat a 6 Figure income

ANTHONY SEGIL

PHIL ZAIKOVATYY

Contents

Foreward

If you're ready to dive into the world of real estate investing and make a fortune, you've come to the right place. This isn't your typical dry, boring real estate manual - we're here to have some fun while we learn the ins and outs of building a profitable rental property empire in the Golden State. So, buckle up, because we're about to embark on an exciting, laughter-filled journey to financial success!

Have you ever dreamt of becoming a real estate mogul, sipping piña coladas on the beach while the rent checks roll in? In this book, we'll take a humorous, no-nonsense approach to help you achieve that dream. We'll explore the unique opportunities offered by accessory dwelling units (ADUs) and junior accessory dwelling units (JADUs) in California, showing you how to maximize your rental income while minimizing your headaches. From finding the perfect properties to managing tenants and navigating the state's ever-changing landlord-tenant laws, we've got you covered.

As you progress through the chapters, you'll learn the secrets of successful landlording, including the art of negotiation, mastering maintenance, and marketing your rental units. We'll share hilarious stories of real-life landlord hiccups and show you how to handle even the most challenging situations with humor and grace. And, of course, we'll discuss the endgame: building a real estate empire that allows you to retire early and enjoy the fruits of your labor.

This book is designed for aspiring landlords who want to learn the ropes in a fun, engaging way. We'll provide you with all the tools, tips, and tricks you need to succeed, while keeping things light and entertaining. Whether you're an experienced investor or a complete newbie, you'll find something of value in these pages. So grab your favorite beverage, kick back, and get ready to laugh your way to financial freedom!

Why Investing In California Real Estate Is Smart

The California real estate market has consistently proven itself as an attractive investment option for both domestic and international investors. With its strong economy, diverse industries, growing population, and high-quality properties, the Golden State offers numerous opportunities for those looking to invest in real estate. Here are several key reasons why investing in California real estate is a smart move:

1. Population Growth and Demand: As the most populous state in the United States, California's population is estimated at over 44 million in 2025, with projections to reach 48 million by 2050, according to the California Department of Finance. This steady population growth creates a strong demand for housing, making the real estate market an appealing investment option.

2. Economic Powerhouse: California's economy ranks as the world's fifth-largest, with a GDP of approximately $3.3 trillion in 2022. The state is home to a diverse range of industries, including technology, entertainment, agriculture, and tourism. This economic strength contributes to a resilient real estate market, ensuring that demand

for both residential and commercial properties remains robust.

3. Job Opportunities: California has led the nation in job creation, adding over 3.3 million jobs since 2010. The state's thriving tech industry in Silicon Valley, the entertainment sector in Los Angeles, and the startup scene in cities like San Francisco and San Diego create a healthy job market. High-income job opportunities drive demand for housing, making real estate investments in California even more attractive.

4. Housing Appreciation: The California real estate market has experienced significant appreciation in the past decade. According to Zillow, the median home value in the state increased by approximately 96% between 2015 and 2022, outperforming the national average. This impressive growth in home values demonstrates the potential for capital gains when investing in California real estate.

5. High Rental Yields: Despite rent control measures in certain cities, California's rental market offers attractive returns for property investors. The U.S. Census Bureau reported that the median gross rent in California was $2,274 in 2022, significantly higher than the national median of $1,600. Additionally, Zumper indicated that the statewide median rent for a one-bedroom apartment increased by approximately 40% between 2015 and 2022.

These factors contribute to strong rental yields and consistent rental income for investors.

6. Positive Market Outlook: The state's strong economy, diverse industries, and population growth suggest continued growth in housing values and rental rates, offering long-term stability and attractive returns for real estate investors.

In conclusion, investing in the California real estate market is a smart move due to its booming population, strong economy, thriving job market, impressive housing appreciation, high rental yields, and promising market outlook. Investors seeking to capitalize on these trends and diversify their portfolios should consider the Golden State's real estate market as a valuable addition to their investment strategy.

Chapter 1:
Finding Your Inner Mogul:
The Landlord Mindset

1. Embracing the entrepreneurial spirit If you've ever watched a reality TV show about real estate moguls, you might think that they were born with a golden key to success. The truth is, anyone can become a landlord extraordinaire – it just takes the right mindset and a willingness to take risks (and a healthy dose of humor, of course). Real estate investing isn't for the faint of heart, but if you're willing to roll up your sleeves and dive in headfirst, the rewards can be substantial. So put on your mogul hat, and let's get down to business!

2. Developing a winning mindset. Aspiring landlords, take note: a positive attitude and solution-oriented mindset are the keys to success in the world of real estate investing. Instead of seeing obstacles as insurmountable, learn to view them as opportunities for growth and improvement. And when things don't go as planned (which they inevitably will), remember to laugh it off and learn from your mistakes. After all, Rome wasn't built in a day, and neither will your real estate empire.

3. Setting SMART goals for your real estate empire. Ready to start building your empire? Before you jump in, take some time to set clear, achievable goals that will guide you on your journey. Make sure your goals are SMART: Specific, Measurable, Achievable, Relevant, and Time-bound. For example, instead of vaguely stating, "I want to be a successful landlord," try setting a goal like, "I will purchase and rent out three properties within the next two years." And don't forget to track your progress along the way – after all, it's hard to celebrate your victories if you don't know what they are!

4. Building a strong support network. No man (or woman) is an island, especially in the world of real estate investing. Surround yourself with like-minded individuals who share your goals and vision, and don't be afraid to ask for help or advice when you need it. The collective wisdom of your network can be a goldmine of information – not to mention a source of hilarious landlord stories to keep you entertained during those late-night maintenance calls.

5. Prioritizing self-care and work-life balance. Becoming a successful landlord isn't just about raking in the cash – it's also about maintaining a healthy work-life balance. Make sure to carve out time for relaxation, hobbies, and personal interests, and don't let your real estate empire consume your entire life. After all, what's the point of becoming a wealthy landlord if you're too stressed and

burnt out to enjoy your success? Remember, laughter is the best medicine, so make sure to have a healthy dose of humor in your daily life.

With the right mindset, a clear plan, and a supportive network, you'll be well on your way to laughing all the way to the bank as a successful landlord in California. So, buckle up and get ready for the ride of your life – it's time to start building your real estate empire!

Chapter 2:

California Dreamin': Navigating the Golden State's Real Estate Market

1. Understanding the unique aspects of California's real estate market. The California real estate market is like a box of chocolates – you never know what you're going to get (but you can bet it'll be expensive!). High property values, combined with the allure of living in a land of movie stars and perfect weather, make the Golden State a prime location for real estate investing. But beware: this sun-kissed paradise comes with its fair share of challenges, including wildfires and earthquakes. So, grab your surfboard and your fire extinguisher, and let's dive into the wild world of California real estate!

2. Researching and identifying profitable markets and neighborhoods. Location, location, location – it's the real estate mantra for a reason. In order to maximize your rental income, you'll need to identify the most lucrative markets and neighborhoods in California. Start by researching local rental rates, property values, and economic trends, and keep an eye out for up-and-coming areas that are ripe for investment. And while you're at it, don't forget to take a moment to enjoy the sunshine and

savor the local cuisine (after all, who can resist a California burrito?).

3. The secret sauce: finding undervalued properties with potential Finding undervalued properties in California is like searching for a needle in a haystack – or more accurately, a single avocado in a mountain of guacamole. But fear not, intrepid investors! With some savvy sleuthing and a bit of luck, you can uncover hidden gems in even the most competitive markets. Start by leveraging online resources, such as property listing websites and local real estate forums, and don't be shy about networking with local real estate professionals. Remember, fortune favors the bold (and the well-informed!).

4. Timing the market: when to buy and when to hold Ah, the age-old question: to buy, or not to buy? Timing the real estate market can feel like trying to catch a wave on a surfboard made of Jell-O, but there are some general principles to keep in mind. First, it's important to recognize that attempting to time the market is inherently risky, and there are no guarantees of success. Instead of trying to predict the next big boom or bust, focus on identifying market trends and making informed investment decisions based on your research and financial goals. And if all else fails, you can always consult your trusty Magic 8-Ball (results may vary).

5. The role of humor in navigating California's real estate market. Let's face it: investing in California real estate can be a rollercoaster ride of emotions, from the thrill of finding a great deal to the heartbreak of losing out on your dream property. One thing's for sure, though – a healthy sense of humor can help you navigate the ups and downs with grace and resilience. So, don't be afraid to laugh at the absurdity of it all, and remember that even the most successful investors have their fair share of hilarious (and humbling) stories to tell. After all, as the old saying goes, "If you don't laugh, you'll cry."

With a solid understanding of California's unique real estate market and a willingness to embrace the challenges (and the laughs) that come with it, you'll be well on your way to building a profitable rental property empire in the Golden State. So, slap on some sunscreen and grab your shades – it's time to hit the beach and start California dreamin'!

Chapter 3:
The JADU and ADU Advantage:
How to Maximize Your Rental Income

1. The ADU and JADU revolution. If you're looking to maximize your rental income, accessory dwelling units (ADUs) and junior accessory dwelling units (JADUs) are the way to go. Think of them as the avocado toast of California real estate – trendy, versatile, and oh-so-profitable. These compact living spaces can be added to your existing property, providing an additional source of income without the need to purchase an entirely new piece of real estate. So, let's explore the wonderful world of ADUs and JADUs, and learn how to make them work for you.

2. Understanding the differences between ADUs and JADUs. ADUs and JADUs may sound like they belong in a galaxy far, far away, but they're just two different types of accessory dwelling units. In a nutshell, ADUs are stand-alone structures that are generally under 1200 sq. feet. (think backyard granny flats), while JADUs are smaller, self-contained living spaces carved out of an existing home or garages. Each option has its pros and cons, but

both can be a fantastic way to boost your rental income and make the most of your property's potential.

3. Navigating California's ADU and JADU regulations - Like a stubborn burrito that refuses to be wrapped, California's ADU and JADU regulations can be a bit tricky to navigate. But don't worry – we're here to help you untangle the red tape and make sense of it all. First, familiarize yourself with California's statewide ADU and JADU laws, which set the basic guidelines for permitting and construction. Then, consult your local city or county ordinances for any additional requirements or restrictions that may apply in your area. And if you're feeling overwhelmed, remember that a little humor goes a long way – after all, laughter is the best weapon against bureaucratic frustration.

4. Designing and building your ADU or JADU. Building an ADU or JADU is like assembling a jigsaw puzzle – it takes patience, creativity, and a keen eye for detail. Start by evaluating your property's layout and determining the best location for your new unit, keeping in mind factors like privacy, access, and available space. Then, consult with an architect or contractor to design a functional, attractive living space that meets all local building codes and regulations. Remember, an ounce of planning is worth a pound of cure (or in this case, a ton of rent money).

5. Attracting tenants and maximizing your rental income. Once your ADU or JADU is built, it's time to find the perfect tenants and start raking in the dough. Consider offering competitive rental rates and attractive amenities to make your unit stand out from the competition, and don't be afraid to flex your marketing muscles. And, of course, don't forget to inject a little humor into the process – a funny "For Rent" sign or a clever online listing can go a long way in attracting potential renters and making your property memorable.

By harnessing the power of ADUs and JADUs, you can unlock new streams of rental income and elevate your real estate game to new heights. So, put on your hard hat, grab your blueprints, and let's get ready to build your way to financial success in California!

Chapter 4:

The Art of Tenant-ology: Mastering the Landlord-Tenant Relationship

1. The importance of finding the right tenants. They say that good fences make good neighbors, but we say that great tenants make even better renters. The key to a successful landlord-tenant relationship is finding the perfect match – someone who will treat your property with respect, pay rent on time, and perhaps even share your affinity for dad jokes. To find your ideal renter, you'll need a combination of thorough screening, a keen intuition, and a little bit of luck. So, buckle up and get ready to channel your inner Sherlock Holmes – it's time to embark on the great tenant hunt!

2. Crafting an irresistible rental listing. The first step in attracting your dream tenant is creating a rental listing that's equal parts informative, enticing, and, of course, hilarious. Start by highlighting your property's best features and amenities, and then throw in a few witty one-liners or puns to keep your potential renters entertained. After all, laughter is the best icebreaker, and a funny listing can help set the stage for a positive landlord-tenant relationship from day one.

3. The art of tenant screening. Tenant screening is a bit like speed dating – it's all about making quick, informed decisions based on limited information. Begin by reviewing each applicant's credit report, rental history, and references, and trust your gut instincts when it comes to red flags or potential compatibility issues. Remember, it's better to be thorough and patient than to rush into a rental agreement with the wrong tenant. And if you find yourself feeling overwhelmed, just imagine the hilarious stories you'll have to share at your next landlord support group meeting.

4. Building rapport and setting boundaries. Once you've found your perfect tenant, it's important to maintain open lines of communication and set clear expectations from the start. While a little humor can go a long way in fostering a positive relationship, it's also crucial to strike a balance between being approachable and maintaining professional boundaries. Think of yourself as the Mary Poppins of landlords – firm but fair, with a touch of whimsy and a dash of sarcasm.

5. Handling maintenance and repairs with a smile. As a landlord, you'll inevitably have to deal with maintenance requests and repairs – it's all part of the job. Instead of dreading these tasks, learn to embrace them as opportunities to flex your problem-solving skills and showcase your sense of humor. Whether you're unclogging a stubborn toilet or patching a leaky roof, a can-do attitude and

a well-timed joke can help ease tensions and keep your tenants satisfied. Just remember to keep a plumber on speed dial – you never know when you'll need a backup plan (or a good laugh).

By mastering the art of tenant-ology, you can build strong, lasting relationships with your renters and create a harmonious, profitable rental experience for everyone involved. So, polish up your people skills, brush up on your dad jokes, and get ready to become the landlord your tenants will brag about at their next dinner party!

Chapter 5:
The Landlord's Survival Guide: Tackling Legal Issues and Keeping Your Sanity

1. Staying on top of landlord-tenant laws. As a landlord in California, you'll need to navigate a labyrinth of laws and regulations designed to protect both you and your tenants. While it may seem overwhelming at first, staying informed and compliant is crucial to avoiding legal headaches down the road. So, pour yourself a strong cup of coffee (or something stronger, if that's your preference) and immerse yourself in the thrilling world of landlord-tenant law. Remember, knowledge is power – and humor is the best coping mechanism.

2. Crafting a rock-solid lease agreement. A well-written lease agreement is like a warm hug – it provides comfort, security, and a clear understanding of expectations. Take the time to create a comprehensive, legally compliant lease that covers everything from rent and security deposits to maintenance responsibilities and pet policies. And while you're at it, don't be afraid to inject a little personality into the document – after all, who says legal contracts can't be entertaining? Just be sure to consult

with a qualified attorney to ensure your lease is up to snuff.

3. Managing security deposits and rent collection. As much as we'd love to believe that money grows on trees (or in this case, rental properties), the reality is that rent collection and security deposit management can be a bit of a headache. Set clear policies and expectations for rent payments and late fees and consider using on-line platforms to streamline the process. When it comes to security deposits, follow California's guidelines to ensure you're in compliance with state laws. And if disputes arise, try to keep your cool and use humor to diffuse tense situations – laughter can be a powerful mediator.

4. Dealing with difficult tenants and evictions. Despite your best efforts to screen and select the perfect renters, there's always a chance you'll encounter a difficult tenant or two along the way. From late rent payments to noise complaints, the key to handling challenging situations is a combination of firmness, fairness, and a hearty dose of humor. When all else fails, you may need to consider the dreaded "E" word – eviction. Make sure to follow California's eviction laws to the letter and consult with an attorney to ensure you're on solid legal ground.

5. Maintaining your sense of humor (and sanity) in the face of adversity Let's face it: being a landlord can be a stressful, thankless job at times. But with a little resilience and

a lot of humor, you can tackle even the most daunting challenges with grace and style. Remember to laugh at the absurdity of it all and learn from your experiences – after all, every setback is just another opportunity for growth (and a great anecdote to share at your next dinner party). So, take a deep breath, crack a smile, and get ready to face the world of landlording with courage and a healthy dose of laughter.

Armed with a solid understanding of the legal landscape and a well-honed sense of humor, you'll be well-equipped to tackle any challenges that come your way as a California landlord. Just remember to stay informed, stay flexible, and above all, stay hilarious – your tenants (and your sanity) will thank you.

Chapter 6:

The Taxman Cometh: Navigating Taxes and Expenses Like a Pro

1. Understanding rental income taxation. Taxes may be one of the few certainties in life, but that doesn't mean they have to be a source of dread and despair. As a landlord, you'll need to report your rental income to the taxman, so it's essential to understand the ins and outs of the process. With a little research, a lot of patience, and a hearty dose of humor, you can transform tax season from a nightmare into a mildly amusing challenge. After all, who doesn't love a good tax-related pun?

2. Deduct, deduct, deduct. When it comes to rental property taxes, deductions are your best friends. From mortgage interest and property taxes to repairs and maintenance, there are a plethora of expenses that can help offset your taxable income. So, channel your inner detective and start hunting for deductions – just be sure to keep meticulous records and consult with a tax professional to ensure you're maximizing your savings (and staying on the right side of the law).

3. Depreciation: turning lemons into lemonade. Depreciation may sound like a bummer, but it's actually a sweet

tax-saving opportunity for landlords. By depreciating the value of your rental property over time, you can reduce your taxable income and save money in the long run. So, grab your calculator, brush up on your math skills, and prepare to embrace the wonderful world of depreciation. Just remember to consult with a tax expert to ensure you're applying the rules correctly – nobody wants an angry letter from the IRS.

4. Keeping track of expenses and records. If you're a landlord, keeping track of expenses and records is like flossing – it's not the most exciting task, but it's essential for maintaining your financial health. Invest in a solid record-keeping system, whether it's a trusty filing cabinet or a cutting-edge software program and make a habit of updating it regularly. And while you're at it, why not have some fun with it? Jazz up your spreadsheets with colorful fonts or create a humorous filing system based on your favorite sitcom characters. The possibilities are endless (and mildly entertaining).

5. Seeking professional help (and comic relief). Navigating the complexities of rental property taxes can be a daunting task, even for the most seasoned landlords. If you're feeling overwhelmed or unsure, don't hesitate to seek the help of a qualified tax professional. Not only can they provide expert guidance and advice, but they may even share a few tax-related jokes to brighten your

day. After all, laughter is the best medicine – especially when it comes to curing the tax-season blues.

By staying organized, leveraging deductions, and keeping your sense of humor intact, you can conquer your rental property taxes like a true pro. So, slap on your "World's Best Landlord" hat, sharpen your pencils, and get ready to tackle the taxman with confidence and a smile!

Chapter 7:
The Zen of Property Maintenance: Keeping Your Rentals Shipshape and Your Tenants Happy

1. Embracing a proactive approach. When it comes to property maintenance, an ounce of prevention is worth a pound of cure – or in this case, a mountain of repair bills. Adopting a proactive mindset can help you stay ahead of potential issues, saving you time, money, and stress in the long run. So, channel your inner Mr. Miyagi and embrace the art of preventive maintenance. Wax on, wax off, and keep those rentals in tip-top shape!

2. Creating a maintenance schedule. A well-organized maintenance schedule is like a finely tuned orchestra – each element works in harmony to create a beautiful symphony of upkeep. Develop a system that includes routine inspections, seasonal tasks, and long-term maintenance projects to ensure your property stays in peak condition year-round. And don't forget to throw in a few comedic curveballs – after all, laughter is the grease that keeps the wheels of property management turning.

3. Building a reliable team of professionals. As a landlord, you'll need a crack team of professionals to help keep

your properties running smoothly – think of them as your maintenance Avengers. From plumbers and electricians to landscapers and pest control experts, these skilled workers are essential for tackling repairs and maintenance tasks beyond your DIY abilities. So, assemble your team, forge strong relationships, and prepare to conquer the world of property maintenance with a smile and a well-timed joke.

4. Fostering open communication with tenants. Maintaining a rental property is a team effort, and your tenants play a crucial role in keeping everything shipshape. Encourage open communication and create an environment where they feel comfortable reporting maintenance issues or concerns. A little humor can go a long way in fostering this sense of camaraderie – after all, who wouldn't want to report a leaky faucet to a landlord with a penchant for plumbing puns?

5. Handling emergencies with grace (and a dash of humor). As much as we'd like to believe that rental properties are immune to disasters, the reality is that emergencies can (and will) happen. When faced with a crisis, it's essential to stay calm, act swiftly, and maintain a sense of humor to help ease tensions and keep your tenants reassured. Whether you're dealing with a burst pipe or a swarm of angry bees, a level-headed approach and a well-timed joke can make all the difference.

By adopting a proactive approach to property maintenance and fostering a positive relationship with your tenants, you can keep your rentals in tip-top shape and ensure a harmonious living environment for everyone involved. So, roll up your sleeves, grab your toolbelt, and get ready to tackle the world of property upkeep with a smile and a hearty dose of humor!

Chapter 8:

Location, Location, Laughter: Making the Most of Your Rental Property's Locale

1. Embracing the quirks of your neighborhood. Every neighborhood has its own unique personality – from the bustling urban jungle to the tranquil suburban oasis. As a landlord, it's essential to embrace the quirks and charms of your rental property's locale and use them to your advantage. Highlight the best features of the area in your rental listings, and don't be afraid to throw in a few lighthearted observations or jokes. After all, laughter is a universal language that transcends zip codes and time zones.

2. Staying informed and involved. As a landlord, it's important to stay informed about local events, developments, and issues that could impact your rental property or tenants. Attend community meetings, read neighborhood newsletters, and consider joining local organizations to stay in the loop. A strong sense of community involvement can not only help you stay abreast of local happenings but also provide ample opportunities

for networking and comic relief. Who knows, you might even become the unofficial neighborhood mascot!

3. Capitalizing on local amenities. From parks and public transportation to schools and shopping centers, local amenities can play a significant role in attracting (and retaining) tenants. Be sure to highlight these features in your rental listings and conversations with prospective renters. And while you're at it, why not have a little fun with it? Create a humorous "Top 10" list of neighborhood perks, or craft a tongue-in-cheek map of the area's hidden gems. A little creativity and humor can go a long way in showcasing your rental property's appeal.

4. Building strong relationships with neighbors. Good neighbors are worth their weight in gold – or in this case, rental income. Building strong relationships with the people who live near your rental property can help create a sense of community and provide invaluable support in times of need. So, get to know your neighbors, share a laugh or two, and work together to create a harmonious living environment for all. Just remember to keep the dad jokes to a minimum – not everyone shares your impeccable taste in humor.

5. Embracing the power of local marketing When it comes to marketing your rental property, sometimes the best approach is to think globally and act locally. Consider partnering with local businesses, participating in

community events, or even sponsoring a neighborhood sports team to increase your property's visibility and appeal. And don't be afraid to inject a little humor into your marketing efforts – a funny billboard or a clever social media campaign can help set your rental property apart from the competition.

By embracing the unique charms of your rental property's locale and forging strong connections with neighbors and community members, you can create a welcoming, vibrant living environment that attracts and retains high-quality tenants. So, put on your explorer's hat, dust off your joke book, and set out on a journey to discover the laughter-filled world that lies just beyond your front door.

Chapter 9:
The Art of Tenant Relations: Building Trust, Loyalty, and a Dash of Fun

1. The power of a warm welcome. They say you never get a second chance to make a first impression, and when it comes to tenant relations, truer words have never been spoken. Start your landlord-tenant relationship on the right foot with a warm, personalized welcome – whether it's a handwritten note, a small gift, or a hilarious joke to break the ice. This simple gesture can set the tone for a positive, friendly, and mutually beneficial partnership.

2. Communication is key (and comedy is the master key). In the world of tenant relations, communication is the lifeblood that keeps everything running smoothly. Try to stay in regular contact with your tenants, providing updates on maintenance, neighborhood news, and any other relevant information. And while you're at it, don't be afraid to sprinkle in a little humor – a well-timed pun or witty anecdote can help keep your communications lighthearted and engaging.

3. Respecting privacy and boundaries. While maintaining open lines of communication is essential, it's equally important to respect your tenants' privacy and boundaries.

Avoid showing up unannounced or making intrusive requests, and always give plenty of notice before entering the property for inspections or repairs. And if you're ever in doubt, just remember the Golden Rule of Landlording: treat your tenants as you would like to be treated (ideally with a healthy dose of laughter and respect).

4. Addressing concerns and complaints with grace (and a touch of humor) No matter how diligent you are as a landlord, issues and concerns will inevitably arise. When they do, it's essential to address them promptly, professionally, and with a touch of humor to help diffuse any tension. Whether you're dealing with a noise complaint, a maintenance issue, or a disagreement over the security deposit, a level-headed approach and a well-timed joke can work wonders in resolving conflicts and maintaining a positive landlord-tenant relationship.

5. Celebrating milestones and building loyalty. In the world of rental properties, tenant loyalty is the holy grail – a coveted prize that can save you time, money, and stress in the long run. To help foster this sense of loyalty, consider celebrating important milestones, such as lease renewals, with small tokens of appreciation or humorous gestures. A funny card, a modest gift, or even a heartfelt "thank you" can go a long way in making your tenants feel valued and appreciated.

By embracing the art of tenant relations and injecting a healthy dose of humor into your interactions, you can create a positive, supportive living environment that keeps your renters happy and your rental income flowing. So, don your comedy cap, brush up on your dad jokes, and get ready to become the world's funniest – and most successful – landlord!

Chapter 10:

The Fine Art of Rent Collection: Balancing Firmness, Flexibility, and Funniness

1. Establishing clear payment expectations. In the world of landlording, rent collection is the main event – the grand finale that brings your hard work and dedication to fruition. To ensure a smooth and seamless process, it's essential to establish clear payment expectations from the get-go. Make sure your lease agreement outlines the rent amount, due date, and any applicable late fees or penalties. And while you're at it, consider adding a light-hearted note or joke to keep the tone friendly and approachable – after all, laughter is the best currency (or something like that).

2. Offering convenient payment options. In today's fast-paced, digital world, convenience is king – and rent collection is no exception. Offer your tenants a variety of payment options, such as online transfers, direct deposit, or even mobile payment apps, to make the process as hassle-free as possible. And for those old-school renters who still prefer to pay by check or cash, consider setting up a secure drop-off location or mailing system. Just

be sure to provide clear instructions, and maybe even a humorous how-to guide to ensure everyone's on the same page.

3. Maintaining a firm but flexible approach. While it's important to be firm when it comes to rent collection, it's equally crucial to maintain a sense of flexibility and understanding. Life happens, and sometimes tenants may encounter unexpected financial hardships or personal challenges. In these situations, consider working with them to create a payment plan or temporary arrangement that meets both parties' needs. A little empathy and a well-timed joke can go a long way in maintaining a positive landlord-tenant relationship during challenging times.

4. Keeping records and staying organized. When it comes to rent collection, organization is your secret weapon – the key to unlocking a smooth and stress-free process. Invest in a reliable record-keeping system, whether it's a spreadsheet, software program, or old-fashioned ledger, and make a habit of updating it regularly. And while you're at it, why not add a little humor to the mix? Create a funny rent collection calendar or give each tenant a quirky nickname to liven up your records.

5. Navigating late payments and evictions with tact (and a touch of comedy). Despite your best efforts, there may come a time when you're faced with a late payment or

even the prospect of eviction. In these situations, it's essential to remain professional, empathetic, and firm in your approach. Communicate with your tenant to understand the issue and explore potential solutions, and don't be afraid to use humor to help diffuse tensions and maintain a positive rapport. If all else fails, consult with a legal professional to ensure you're following the appropriate steps and procedures for your jurisdiction.

By balancing firmness, flexibility, and a healthy dose of humor, you can master the fine art of rent collection and create a positive, mutually beneficial relationship with your tenants. So, grab your calculator, dust off your joke book, and get ready to collect those rents with a smile and a chuckle!

Chapter 11:
Landlord Superpowers: Juggling Finances, Time Management, and Comic Relief

1. Mastering the financial juggling act. In the world of land-lording, money management is a vital skill – one that requires a delicate balance of thriftiness, foresight, and financial acumen. To keep your rental empire running smoothly, create a detailed budget, track expenses, and stay vigilant for opportunities to reduce costs or increase revenue. And while you're at it, why not inject a little humor into the process? Share your favorite money-related jokes or create a lighthearted financial vision board to keep things fun and engaging.

2. Time management for the multitasking landlord. As a landlord, you'll need to wear many hats – property manager, maintenance guru, tenant liaison, and more. To juggle these responsibilities effectively, it's essential to hone your time management skills and prioritize tasks based on their urgency and importance. And when the going gets tough, remember that laughter is the best medicine – a well-timed joke or humorous anecdote can help ease stress and keep your spirits high.

3. Delegating tasks and building a support team. Even the most skilled and dedicated landlord can't do it all alone. To lighten your workload and streamline your operations, consider delegating tasks to a trusted team of professionals or support staff. From property managers and maintenance workers to financial advisors and legal consultants, these experts can help you navigate the complex world of landlording with ease and efficiency. Just be sure to keep the humor flowing – after all, a shared laugh can be a powerful team-building tool.

4. Staying organized in the face of chaos. In the fast-paced, ever-changing world of rental properties, organization is your secret weapon – the key to staying one step ahead of the curve. Develop a comprehensive record-keeping system, create a property management calendar, and establish routines to help you stay organized and on top of your game. And don't be afraid to infuse a little humor into the mix – a comical filing system or a lighthearted to-do list can help make even the most mundane tasks more enjoyable.

5. Embracing the power of self-care and humor. As a landlord, it's essential to prioritize your well-being and make time for self-care. Regular exercise, a healthy diet, and plenty of rest are vital for maintaining the physical and mental stamina needed to excel in the world of property management. And don't forget the healing power of laughter – whether it's a funny podcast, a comedy show,

or a hilarious conversation with a tenant, a good chuckle can work wonders for your mood and overall outlook.

By mastering the art of juggling finances, time management, and comic relief, you can transform yourself into a landlord superhero – a property management powerhouse with the skills, knowledge, and wit to conquer any challenge that comes your way. So, strap on your cape, polish your punchlines, and get ready to soar to new heights in the world of landlording!

Chapter 12:
The Unexpected Adventures of Landlording: Dealing with Surprises and Laughter in the Face of Adversity

1. Embracing the element of surprise. In the world of land-lording, the unexpected is practically a job requirement – from leaky pipes and late-night lockouts to pesky pests and impromptu inspections. To thrive in this unpredict-able environment, it's essential to embrace the element of surprise and develop a strong sense of adaptability. And when faced with adversity, remember that laughter is the best coping mechanism – a well-timed joke or a hearty chuckle can help diffuse tension and put things in perspective.

2. Building a "Landlord Emergency Kit". To navigate the twists and turns of rental property management, it's wise to have a few tricks up your sleeve – or in this case, a "Landlord Emergency Kit" stocked with essential tools, resources, and a healthy dose of humor. From a trusty toolbox and a list of reliable contractors to a stash of funny stories and ice-breaker jokes, this all-in-one sur-vival kit can help you tackle any challenge with grace, grit, and a smile on your face.

3. Cultivating a problem-solving mindset. When faced with an unexpected issue or setback, it's important to approach the situation with a problem-solving mindset. This means staying calm, focused, and resourceful – and, of course, maintaining your sense of humor. By cultivating this can-do attitude, you can transform obstacles into opportunities and make even the most challenging situations more manageable (and maybe even a little bit funny).

4. Learning from experience and growing as a landlord. The unexpected adventures of landlording can be valuable learning experiences – opportunities to grow, adapt, and refine your skills as a property manager. Take the time to reflect on each situation, identify key lessons, and implement improvements to prevent similar issues from arising in the future. And don't be afraid to find the humor in your experiences – sharing your landlord "war stories" can provide comic relief and valuable insights for fellow property owners.

5. Staying resilient and finding joy in the journey. The road to landlording success is rarely a straight, smooth path – it's filled with twists, turns, and the occasional comedic mishap. To thrive in this dynamic environment, it's essential to stay resilient, adaptable, and open to the unexpected. By finding joy in the journey and embracing the power of laughter, you can transform even the most

challenging situations into opportunities for growth, learning, and, of course, a good chuckle.

So, buckle up, put on your comedy armor, and get ready to embark on the wild, unpredictable, and laughter-filled adventure that is landlording. With a positive attitude, a problem-solving mindset, and a healthy dose of humor, there's no challenge you can't overcome and no surprise you can't face with a smile.

Chapter 13:
The Landlord's Guide to Networking: Making Connections, Sharing Laughs, and Building Your Empire

1. The value of a strong network. In the world of landlording, a robust network can be your secret weapon – the key to unlocking valuable resources, support, and opportunities. From fellow property owners and industry professionals to local business owners and potential tenants, these connections can help you stay informed, navigate challenges, and grow your rental empire. And the best part? Building your network can be a fun, laughter-filled experience that adds an extra dose of enjoyment to your landlording journey.

2. Attending industry events and workshops with a smile (and a joke). One of the most effective ways to expand your network is by attending industry events, workshops, and meetups. These gatherings offer invaluable opportunities to learn, connect, and share experiences with fellow landlords and professionals. To make the most of these events, approach them with a positive attitude, an open mind, and, of course, a well-stocked arsenal of

jokes and ice-breakers to keep the conversations light and engaging.

3. Building connections through social media and online forums. In today's digital age, social media and online forums have become indispensable networking tools – virtual platforms where landlords can connect, collaborate, and share a virtual laugh from the comfort of their own homes. Join relevant groups and forums, engage in discussions, and don't be afraid to showcase your humorous side – a well-timed meme or witty comment can work wonders in building rapport and forging lasting connections.

4. Cultivating local relationships and partnerships. While online networking is essential, it's equally important to nurture local relationships and partnerships. Get involved in your community, attend neighborhood events, and consider joining local business associations or chambers of commerce. By fostering these connections, you can tap into a wealth of local knowledge, resources, and support – and maybe even share a few laughs over coffee or at a community gathering.

5. The power of reciprocity and humor in networking. In the world of networking, the old adage "you scratch my back, I'll scratch yours" rings true. Be generous with your time, resources, and knowledge – and don't be afraid to ask for help or advice when needed. This spirit

of reciprocity can help build trust, camaraderie, and a sense of mutual support among your network. And don't forget the power of laughter – a shared joke or humorous anecdote can create a lasting bond and make even the most daunting networking experience more enjoyable.

By embracing the art of networking and harnessing the power of laughter, you can create a thriving, supportive community of connections that will help you navigate the ups and downs of the landlording world. So, put on your networking hat, polish your best jokes, and get ready to make connections, share laughs, and build your rental empire one relationship at a time.

Chapter 14:
The Landlord's Retirement Plan: Building Your Legacy and Laughing All the Way to the Bank

1. Planning for the future with a smile on your face. As a landlord, it's essential to plan for the future and consider how your rental empire can provide long-term financial security and a comfortable retirement. With strategic planning, sound investments, and a healthy dose of humor, you can build a legacy that will have you laughing all the way to the bank. So, grab your financial planner, dust off your joke book, and get ready to map out your path to a prosperous and laughter-filled future.

2. Diversifying your property portfolio. In the world of property investing, diversification is the name of the game. By spreading your investments across various property types, locations, and market segments, you can mitigate risk, maximize returns, and create a well-rounded retirement portfolio. Just be sure to approach the process with a sense of humor and a positive attitude – after all, laughter is the best investment strategy (or at least a close second).

3. Staying informed and adapting to market trends. To ensure your rental empire continues to grow and prosper, it's important to stay informed about market trends and adapt your strategy accordingly. Attend industry events, subscribe to relevant publications, and engage in ongoing education to keep your finger on the pulse of the property market. And don't forget to sprinkle in a little humor – share funny news stories or industry anecdotes to keep things light and enjoyable.

4. Building passive income streams. As you approach retirement, it's wise to focus on building passive income streams that can provide a steady flow of cash without the need for constant hands-on management. This might involve transitioning from active landlording to hiring property managers or exploring alternative investment strategies, such as real estate investment trusts (REITs). Just be sure to approach these changes with a sense of humor – a funny retirement countdown or a lighthearted investment vision board can help keep the process fun and engaging.

5. Leaving a legacy of laughter and financial security. As you build your landlord retirement plan, consider the legacy you'd like to leave behind – not only in terms of financial security but also in the impact you've had on your tenants, community, and fellow landlords. Strive to create a lasting impression of professionalism, compassion, and, of course, humor. By doing so, you can ensure

your legacy will be remembered with a smile – a fitting tribute to a landlord who laughed their way to success.

With strategic planning, adaptability, and a healthy dose of humor, you can build a landlord retirement plan that provides financial security, personal fulfillment, and a legacy of laughter. So, raise a glass (or a rent check) to your future success and get ready to embark on the next chapter of your landlording journey – one filled with prosperity, laughter, and well-earned relaxation.

Chapter 15:

The Landlord's Hall of Fame: Celebrating Your Success and Sharing Your Laughter-Infused Wisdom

1. Recognizing your achievements and milestones. In the world of landlording, success often comes in increments – a property acquired here, a renovation completed there, or a tenant successfully housed. It's essential to take the time to celebrate your achievements, both big and small, as you build your rental empire. Throw a small party, share your milestones on social media, or simply treat yourself to a well-earned pat on the back – and be sure to include a humorous twist to keep the celebrations light and enjoyable.

2. Sharing your laughter-infused wisdom with others. With experience comes wisdom, and as a successful landlord, you have a wealth of knowledge and insights to share with others. Offer advice to new landlords, host workshops, or write articles about your landlording adventures – and don't forget to weave in your trademark humor. Your laughter-infused wisdom can inspire, entertain, and educate others, helping them navigate the world of landlording with a smile on their face.

3. Mentoring the next generation of landlords. As a seasoned landlord, you have a unique opportunity to mentor and support the next generation of property investors. By offering guidance, sharing your experiences, and providing encouragement, you can help others build successful rental empires of their own. And, of course, be sure to pass along your sense of humor – a new landlord armed with a hearty laugh is a force to be reckoned with!

4. Leaving a mark on the industry. Your success as a landlord has the potential to leave a lasting impact on the property management industry. By advocating for best practices, championing positive change, and infusing humor into the sometimes-serious world of landlording, you can help shape the future of property investing for the better. Embrace your role as an industry leader and continue to spread laughter and knowledge throughout your professional community.

5. The Landlord's Hall of Fame: A legacy of laughter and success. As you celebrate your success and share your laughter-infused wisdom, you'll inevitably leave a lasting impression on those around you – tenants, fellow landlords, and industry professionals alike. Your legacy will be one of professionalism, compassion, and, of course, humor – a shining example of what it means to be a successful landlord. Welcome to the Landlord's Hall of Fame, where laughter and success go hand in hand.

With your achievements celebrated and your wisdom shared, your journey as a landlord is far from over. Continue to learn, grow, and find humor in the world of property management, and you'll undoubtedly inspire others to do the same. Here's to a future filled with laughter, success, and a lasting legacy in the Landlord's Hall of Fame!

Chapter 16:

The Landlord's Guide to Work-Life Balance: Juggling Properties and Punchlines

1. Embracing the importance of work-life balance. As a landlord, it's easy to get caught up in the day-to-day responsibilities of managing properties and addressing tenant concerns. However, it's crucial to find a healthy work-life balance that allows you to maintain your sanity, personal relationships, and, of course, your sense of humor. In this chapter, we'll explore strategies for juggling properties and punchlines, ensuring that laughter remains a cornerstone of your landlording experience.

2. Scheduling "me time" and setting boundaries. One of the keys to achieving a healthy work-life balance is carving out time for yourself and setting boundaries between your personal and professional life. Block off time in your schedule for hobbies, relaxation, or spending time with loved ones – and don't forget to include some humor therapy, whether it's watching your favorite comedy or attending a stand-up show. By prioritizing your well-being, you'll be better equipped to manage your rental properties with a clear mind and a light heart.

3. Delegating tasks and outsourcing when necessary. As your rental empire grows, it's important to recognize that you can't do everything on your own. Delegating tasks to property managers, hiring contractors, or outsourcing administrative duties can free up valuable time and energy, allowing you to focus on the aspects of landlording you enjoy most – including sharing jokes and laughter with your tenants and fellow landlords.

4. Building a support network for laughter and encouragement. A strong support network is essential for maintaining a healthy work-life balance. Connect with fellow landlords, friends, and family members who understand the challenges of property management and can offer advice, encouragement, and a listening ear. And don't forget to share your favorite jokes and humorous anecdotes – laughter is a powerful stress-reliever and can help strengthen the bonds within your support network.

5. Maintaining a sense of humor in the face of adversity. As a landlord, you're no stranger to unexpected challenges and setbacks. Maintaining a sense of humor in the face of adversity is crucial for preserving your sanity and bouncing back from difficult situations. When things go awry, take a step back, find the humor in the situation, and remember that laughter is often the best medicine.

By implementing these strategies, you can strike the perfect balance between managing your rental properties and enjoying a fulfilling personal life. So, put on your juggling hat, polish your best punchlines, and get ready to embrace a laughter-filled work-life balance that will keep you smiling, even in the most challenging landlording moments.

Chapter 17:
The Endgame: Building a Real Estate Empire and Retiring Early (With a Laugh, of Course)

1. The joys of early retirement: Leisure, laughter, and landlord legacies The ultimate goal for many landlords is to build a real estate empire that allows them to retire early and enjoy the fruits of their labor. With strategic planning, hard work, and a healthy dose of humor, you can achieve financial independence, retire with a smile on your face, and leave behind a legacy of laughter and success.

2. Setting clear financial goals and timelines (with a side of humor). To retire early, it's essential to set clear financial goals and realistic timelines. Calculate the income you'll need to cover your living expenses and desired lifestyle, and work backward to determine the size and profitability of your real estate portfolio. Add a humorous twist by creating a lighthearted vision board or countdown calendar to keep your goals front and center – and remind you to laugh along the way.

3. Creating a bulletproof investment strategy (and laughing in the face of risk). A sound investment strategy is crucial for building a real estate empire and achieving early retirement. Focus on diversifying your portfolio, optimizing cash flow, and minimizing risk to maximize your returns. And when things don't go as planned, remember to find the humor in the situation – after all, a good laugh can make even the most daunting investment challenges seem more manageable.

4. Automating and delegating for a hands-free approach. As you build your real estate empire and inch closer to early retirement, it's important to transition from hands-on landlord to hands-free investor. Hire property managers, automate administrative tasks, and delegate responsibilities to streamline your operations and free up time for leisure, laughter, and pre-retirement celebrations.

5. Living the dream: Retiring early and enjoying the laughter-filled life you've earned. When you've achieved your financial goals and built a thriving real estate empire, it's time to enjoy the early retirement you've worked so hard for. Embrace your newfound freedom, indulge in your favorite hobbies, and spend quality time with loved ones – all while basking in the laughter and joy that come with a successful landlord legacy.

By focusing on your endgame and infusing humor into every step of the journey, you can build a real estate empire that allows you to retire early and live the laughter-filled life of your dreams. So, raise a glass (or a rent check) to your future success, and get ready to conquer the world of landlording with a smile on your face and a joke up your sleeve.

In Conclusion:
The Last Laugh of the Successful Landlord

As we draw the curtains on this laughter-filled journey through the world of landlording, it's time to reflect on the wisdom, insights, and humorous anecdotes we've shared along the way. From acquiring properties and managing tenants to building a real estate empire and retiring early, this book has explored the many facets of property investing, all while maintaining a lighthearted and humorous tone.

We've discovered that humor is more than just an entertaining diversion in the world of landlording; it's a powerful tool for building relationships, managing stress, and maintaining a healthy work-life balance. By embracing a sense of humor, you can navigate the inevitable challenges of property management with grace, resilience, and, of course, laughter.

As you venture forth to build your own real estate empire, remember to carry the lessons and laughter from this book with you. Share your humorous insights with fellow landlords, regale your tenants with amusing stories, and approach each new challenge with a smile and a chuckle. In doing so, you'll not only create a thriving business but also leave a lasting legacy of laughter and success.

So, raise a glass (or a rent check) one final time to your landlording adventures, and may your journey be filled with prosperity, personal fulfillment, and an endless supply of laughter. After all, the last laugh of the successful landlord is the sweetest one of all.

Happy landlording, and may the punchlines be ever in your favor!

Appendix A:

Breadcrumbs to ROI – A Hilarious Breakdown of True Expenses and Calculations for a Building

In this comical appendix, we'll take a deep dive into the world of ROI calculation by considering the true expenses associated with a building. From profit and interest to depreciation, taxes, and maintenance, we'll provide a step-by-step guide to accurately calculating ROI – all while maintaining our humorous tone.

1. Calculating Profit: Rent and Chuckles

First and foremost, let's determine the annual rental income for your building. Multiply the monthly rent by the number of units and by 12 (months in a year) to find your annual rental income.

Annual Rental Income = Monthly Rent x Number of Units x 12

2. Factoring in Expenses: The Hilarity of Costs

Now, let's incorporate the various expenses associated with your building. These may include:

- Mortgage interest
- Property taxes

- Insurance
- Maintenance and repairs
- Property management fees
- Utilities
- Vacancy allowance

Add up these expenses to calculate your total annual operating expenses.

3. **Accounting for Depreciation: The Amusing Erosion of Value**

Depreciation is the reduction in the value of an asset over time, typically due to wear and tear. For tax purposes, you can depreciate the value of your building (excluding the land) over a period of 27.5 years (for residential properties) or 39 years (for commercial properties).

Annual Depreciation = (Building Value / Depreciation Period)

4. **Computing Net Operating Income (NOI): Profits, Expenses, and Giggles**

To find your building's Net Operating Income (NOI), subtract your total annual operating expenses and annual depreciation from your annual rental income:

NOI = Annual Rental Income - (Total Annual Operating Expenses + Annual Depreciation)

5. Calculating ROI: A Comical Culmination

Finally, to calculate the ROI, divide your NOI by the total investment cost (purchase price + renovation costs + other expenses) and multiply by 100:

ROI = (NOI / Total Investment Cost) x 100

Table A: A Hilarious Example of ROI Calculation with True Expenses

Category	Value
Purchase Price	$ 500,000
Renovation Costs	$ 50,000
Annual Rental Income	$ 60,000
Mortgage Interest	$ 18,000
Property Taxes	$ 6,000
Insurance	$ 2,000
Maintenance	$ 4,000
Property Management	$ 6,000
Utilities	$ 3,000
Vacancy Allowance	$ 3,000
Annual Operating Expenses	$ 42,000
Building Value	$ 450,000

With this delightful example, we've calculated the ROI for a building, incorporating all relevant expenses and deprecia-tion. The result? A comprehensive, accurate, and amusing ROI calculation for your investment property.

By following these breadcrumbs of humor and calculations, you can confidently analyze the true expenses associated with your building and accurately calculate your ROI – all while enjoying a good chuckle along the way. Happy number crunching, and may the laughter be with you!

This laughably meticulous table displays the same ROI calculation as before, only now in a vertical format. Like a stand-up comic delivering a punchline, these values line up one after another for your amusement and financial analysis pleasure. Enjoy the side-splitting excitement of calculating ROI while basking in the hilarity of this reimagined table.

Ah, the delightful world of mortgage notes, principal paydowns, and equity accumulation. In this jolly section, we'll explore the exhilarating concept of mortgage principal paydowns as part of your equity-building strategy. We'll use a hypothetical $200,000 mortgage note at two different interest rates (4% and 5%) to showcase the magic of accumulating equity over time – all while maintaining our humorous, technical writing style.

Let's first calculate the monthly mortgage payments for both interest rates using the good ol' mortgage formula:

Monthly Mortgage Payment = P x (r(1 + r)^n) / ((1 + r)^n - 1)

Where: P = Principal loan amount ($200,000) r = Monthly interest rate (annual rate / 12) n = Number of payments (loan term in years x 12)

Using this formula, we'll calculate the monthly payments for a 30-year mortgage at both 4% and 5% interest rates.

Table 1: Mortgage Payments at Different Interest Rates

Interest Rate	"Monthly Mortgage Payment"
4%	$ 1,479.38
5%	$ 1,581.59

Appendix B:
Real Estate Benefits:
ROI, Depreciation, and
Financial Management

Introduction:

Investing in real estate has long been considered a lucrative and relatively stable form of investment. This sector provides several benefits to investors, including a potential for high returns, tax advantages, and the ability to leverage borrowed capital. In this article, we will discuss key elements of real estate investment, including return on investment (ROI), depreciation, and techniques for calculating returns and expenses in financial management.

1. Return on Investment (ROI):

Return on Investment, or ROI, is a performance metric used to evaluate the profitability of an investment. In real estate, ROI is calculated by dividing the net profit generated by the property by the total amount of money invested. The result is expressed as a percentage, which can be used to compare the performance of various investments.

Formula: ROI = (Net Profit / Investment) x 100

To calculate the net profit, investors need to consider rental income, appreciation, and any other form of revenue generated by the property, while deducting operating expenses, taxes, and maintenance costs.

2. Depreciation:

Depreciation is an accounting method that allocates the cost of a tangible asset over its useful life. In real estate investing, depreciation can provide significant tax benefits by allowing investors to offset a portion of their rental income. For residential properties, the IRS typically uses a 27.5-year depreciation schedule, while commercial properties use a 39-year schedule.

Formula: Depreciation = (Property Value - Land Value) / Depreciation Period

By deducting the depreciation expense from their taxable income, investors can reduce their overall tax liability and increase their net cash flow.

3. Calculating Returns and Expenses:

To effectively manage a real estate investment, investors need to monitor and analyze various financial metrics. Two crucial indicators include the capitalization rate (cap rate) and cash-on-cash return.

a) Capitalization Rate:

The capitalization rate, or cap rate, is a metric that measures the rate of return on a real estate investment based on the income it generates. It is calculated by dividing the property's net operating income (NOI) by its market value.

Formula: Cap Rate = (Net Operating Income / Market Value) x 100

A higher cap rate indicates a higher return on investment and can be useful for comparing the profitability of different properties.

b) Cash-on-Cash Return:

Cash-on-cash return is a measure of the cash income generated by a real estate investment relative to the cash invested. This metric is particularly useful for investors who use leverage (borrowed capital) to finance their properties.

Formula: Cash-on-Cash Return = (Annual Cash Flow / Cash Invested) x 100

This ratio helps investors evaluate the performance of their investments by considering the actual cash inflows relative to the cash invested.

Conclusion:

Understanding ROI, depreciation, and various financial metrics is essential for effective real estate financial management. By calculating and monitoring these indicators, investors can make informed decisions, optimize their investments, and maximize profitability. Proper financial management in real estate investing is key to ensuring long-term success and achieving desired returns.

Appendix C:
Real Estate Investment Examples:
ROI and Cap Rate

Introduction:

To further illustrate the concepts of Return on Investment (ROI) and Capitalization Rate (Cap Rate) in real estate investing, we will provide tangible examples with accompanying charts. These examples will help demonstrate the practical application of these metrics in evaluating the performance of real estate investments.

Example 1: ROI Calculation

Consider an investor who purchases a rental property for $250,000, including acquisition and closing costs. They invest an additional $50,000 in renovations, bringing the total investment to $300,000. The property generates an annual rental income of $30,000, and the annual operating expenses, including taxes, insurance, and maintenance, amount to $10,000.

Net Profit = Rental Income - Operating Expenses Net Profit = $30,000 - $10,000 Net Profit = $20,000

ROI = (Net Profit / Investment) x 100 ROI = ($20,000 / $300,000) x 100 ROI = 6.67%

In this example, the investor's return on investment is 6.67%.

Example 2: Cap Rate Calculation

Consider a commercial property valued at $1,000,000, generating a net operating income (NOI) of $80,000 per year.

Cap Rate = (Net Operating Income / Market Value) x 100 Cap Rate = ($80,000 / $1,000,000) x 100 Cap Rate = 8%

In this example, the capitalization rate for the commercial property is 8%.

Conclusion:

Return on Investment (ROI) and Capitalization Rate (Cap Rate) are critical financial metrics in evaluating real estate investments. By utilizing tangible examples and charts, investors can better understand and apply these concepts in their decision-making process. Ultimately, effective use of these metrics can lead to more informed investment choices, resulting in higher returns and long-term success in real estate investing.

Appendix D:
Real Estate Investment Examples: ROI and Cap Rate

Introduction:

To further illustrate the concepts of Return on Investment (ROI) and Capitalization Rate (Cap Rate) in real estate investing, we will provide tangible examples with accompanying grids. These examples will help demonstrate the practical application of these metrics in evaluating the performance of real estate investments.

Example 1: ROI Calculation

Consider an investor who purchases a rental property for $250,000, including acquisition and closing costs. They invest an additional $50,000 in renovations, bringing the total investment to $300,000. The property generates an annual rental income of $30,000, and the annual operating expenses, including taxes, insurance, and maintenance, amount to $10,000.

Net Profit = Rental Income - Operating Expenses Net Profit = $30,000 - $10,000 Net Profit = $20,000

ROI = (Net Profit / Investment) x 100 ROI = ($20,000 / $300,000) x 100 ROI = 6.67%

In this example, the investor's return on investment is 6.67%.

Example 2: Cap Rate Calculation

Consider a commercial property valued at $1,000,000, generating a net operating income (NOI) of $80,000 per year.

Cap Rate = (Net Operating Income / Market Value) x 100 Cap Rate = ($80,000 / $1,000,000) x 100 Cap Rate = 8%

In this example, the capitalization rate for the commercial property is 8%.

Grid 1: ROI Comparison

The following grid compares the ROI of different real estate investments:

Investment	ROI
A	5%
B (Example 1)	7%
C	8%
D	10%

This grid enables investors to compare the return on investment of different properties, aiding in the decision-making process.

Grid 2: Cap Rate Comparison

The following grid compares the cap rates of various commercial real estate investments:

Property	Cap Rate
A	6%
B	7%
C (Example 2)	8%
D	9%

This grid allows investors to analyze the income-generating potential of different commercial properties, facilitating more informed investment decisions.

Conclusion:

Return on Investment (ROI) and Capitalization Rate (Cap Rate) are critical financial metrics in evaluating real estate investments. By utilizing tangible examples and grids, investors can better understand and apply these concepts in their decision-making process. Ultimately, effective use of these metrics can lead to more informed investment choices, resulting in higher returns and long-term success in real estate investing.

Appendix E:
ROI Calculation with Additional ADU

Introduction:

In this article, we will revisit the previous example of a real estate investment and calculate the Return on Investment (ROI) when an additional Accessory Dwelling Unit (ADU) is added to the property. The ADU generates an additional $18,000 in annual rent, and we will explore how this extra income impacts the overall investment performance.

Example: ROI Calculation with Additional ADU

Recall the initial investment scenario: an investor purchases a rental property for $250,000, including acquisition and closing costs. They invest an additional $50,000 in renovations, bringing the total investment to $300,000. The property generates an annual rental income of $30,000, and the annual operating expenses, including taxes, insurance, and maintenance, amount to $10,000.

With the addition of the ADU, the property generates an extra $18,000 in annual rent, bringing the total rental income to $48,000.

New Rental Income = Original Rental Income + ADU Rental Income New Rental Income = $30,000 + $18,000 New Rental Income = $48,000

Next, we will calculate the new net profit:

New Net Profit = New Rental Income - Operating Expenses New Net Profit = $48,000 - $10,000 New Net Profit = $38,000

Now, we can calculate the new ROI:

New ROI = (New Net Profit / Investment) x 100 New ROI = ($38,000 / $300,000) x 100 New ROI = 12.67%

In this updated scenario, the investor's return on investment increases to 12.67% with the addition of the ADU, which generates an extra $18,000 in annual rent.

Conclusion:

The addition of an Accessory Dwelling Unit (ADU) to an investment property can significantly impact the overall return on investment by increasing rental income. In this example, the ROI increased from 6.67% to 12.67% with the introduction of an ADU. This illustrates the potential benefits of optimizing rental properties to generate higher returns and improve investment performance.

Appendix F:

ROI Calculation with the Addition of an ADU and a Junior ADU

Introduction:

In this article, we will further explore the potential impact of adding both an Accessory Dwelling Unit (ADU) and a Junior Accessory Dwelling Unit (Jr. ADU) to a rental property. We will analyze how the additional rental income from these units affects the overall Return on Investment (ROI) for the property.

Example: ROI Calculation with Additional ADU and Jr. ADU

Let's revisit the original investment scenario: an investor purchases a rental property for $250,000, including acquisition and closing costs. They invest an additional $50,000 in renovations, bringing the total investment to $300,000. The property generates an annual rental income of $30,000, and the annual operating expenses, including taxes, insurance, and maintenance, amount to $10,000.

Suppose the investor can add an ADU that generates an additional $18,000 in annual rent and a Jr. ADU that generates an extra $12,000 in annual rent. The total rental income will now be:

New Rental Income = Original Rental Income + ADU Rental Income + Jr. ADU Rental Income New Rental Income = $30,000 + $18,000 + $12,000 New Rental Income = $60,000

Next, we will calculate the new net profit:

New Net Profit = New Rental Income - Operating Expenses New Net Profit = $60,000 - $10,000 New Net Profit = $50,000

Now, we can calculate the new ROI:

New ROI = (New Net Profit / Investment) x 100 New ROI = ($50,000 / $300,000) x 100 New ROI = 16.67%

In this updated scenario, with the addition of both an ADU and a Jr. ADU, the investor's return on investment increases to 16.67%.

Conclusion:

Adding an Accessory Dwelling Unit (ADU) and a Junior Accessory Dwelling Unit (Jr. ADU) to a rental property can have a significant positive impact on the overall return on investment by providing additional rental income. In the presented example, the ROI increased from 6.67% to 16.67% with the introduction of both an ADU and a Jr. ADU. This demonstrates the potential benefits of optimizing rental properties through the addition of accessory dwelling units, which can lead to higher returns and improved investment performance.

Appendix G:
Spreadsheet for Listing Expense Categories Associated with an Investment Property

Introduction:

In order to effectively manage and track expenses associated with an investment property, it is essential to create a comprehensive spreadsheet. This spreadsheet should list all expense categories related to the property, allowing for easy organization and analysis of financial data. Below, we provide a sample spreadsheet template that can be used to list the expense categories associated with an investment property.

Spreadsheet Template:

Expense Category	Description
Mortgage Payment	Monthly mortgage payment, including principal and interest
Property Taxes	Annual property taxes based on assessed value
Insurance	Annual property insurance premium
Property Management	Monthly fees for property management services
Repairs & Maintenance	Costs for routine maintenance and repairs of the property
Utilities	Monthly utility costs, if not covered by tenants
Landscaping	Costs for landscaping and lawn care services
Pest Control	Expenses for regular pest control services
HOA Fees	Homeowners Association (HOA) fees, if applicable
Legal Accounting	"Legal and accounting fees for professional services"
Marketing Advertising	"Costs for marketing and advertising rental property vacancies"
Leasing Fees	Fees paid to leasing agents for tenant placement
Tenant Screening	Costs associated with screening potential tenants
Eviction Expenses	Legal and administrative expenses related to tenant evictions
Capital Expenditures	Major property improvements and replacements, such as roof, HVAC
Miscellaneous	Other miscellaneous expenses related to the property
Total Expenses	Sum of all expense categories

Conclusion:

A well-organized spreadsheet is essential for managing and tracking the expenses associated with an investment property. By listing all relevant expense categories, investors can easily monitor their property's financial performance and make informed decisions for optimizing their investments. The provided spreadsheet template can be customized to meet individual needs and preferences, ensuring accurate tracking and management of property-related expenses.

Appendix H:
The Impact of Mortgage Principal Reduction on Investment Property Returns

Introduction:

When evaluating the financial performance of an investment property, it is important to consider the impact of mortgage principal reduction on return calculations. A portion of each mortgage payment goes towards paying down the principal balance of the loan, effectively increasing the owner's equity in the property and lowering the amount owed. In this article, we will explore the concept of mortgage principal reduction and its implications for return calculations on investment properties.

Mortgage Principal Reduction and Investment Property Returns:

Each mortgage payment consists of two primary components: principal and interest. The principal portion of the payment reduces the outstanding loan balance, while the interest portion represents the cost of borrowing the funds. As the principal balance decreases over time, the owner's equity in the property increases, leading to potential wealth accumulation.

In the context of an investment property, mortgage principal reduction plays a significant role in the overall return on investment (ROI). While it may not directly contribute to cash flow, principal reduction effectively lowers the amount of debt owed on the property, thereby increasing the owner's net worth. Consequently, the overall ROI for the property should take into account both the cash flow generated from rental income and the increase in equity resulting from mortgage principal reduction.

To account for mortgage principal reduction in the ROI calculation, an adjusted formula can be used:

Adjusted ROI = [(Net Profit + Annual Principal Reduction) / Investment] x 100

Using the previous example:

Investor purchases a rental property for $250,000, including acquisition and closing costs. They invest an additional $50,000 in renovations, bringing the total investment to $300,000. The property generates an annual rental income of $30,000, and the annual operating expenses, including taxes, insurance, and maintenance, amount to $10,000. Let's assume that $4,000 of the annual mortgage payment goes towards principal reduction.

Net Profit = Rental Income - Operating Expenses Net Profit = $30,000 - $10,000 Net Profit = $20,000

Adjusted ROI = [(Net Profit + Annual Principal Reduction) / Investment] x 100 Adjusted ROI = [($20,000 + $4,000) / $300,000] x 100 Adjusted ROI = 8.00%

In this example, when taking mortgage principal reduction into account, the adjusted ROI increases to 8.00%.

Conclusion:

Mortgage principal reduction plays an essential role in the financial performance of investment properties, as it increases the owner's equity and lowers the amount of debt owed. By incorporating mortgage principal reduction into return calculations, investors can gain a more comprehensive understanding of their investment's performance. This adjusted approach to ROI calculation enables investors to make more informed decisions and optimize their investment strategies for long-term success in the real estate market.

Appendix I:
Investment Property
Performance Analysis

Introduction:

A grid can be an effective tool for analyzing the performance of an investment property, as it allows investors to organize and compare various financial metrics. By presenting data in a clear, concise format, a grid enables investors to gain a comprehensive understanding of their investment's performance and make informed decisions. In this article, we will create a grid to analyze the performance of an investment property, incorporating key metrics such as rental income, operating expenses, net profit, and return on investment (ROI).

Investment Property Performance Analysis Grid

Metric	Amount	Description
Purchase Price	$ 250,000	"The acquisition cost of the property, including closing costs"
Renovation Costs	$ 50,000	The cost of property improvements and renovations
Total Investment	$ 300,000	The sum of the purchase price and renovation costs
Annual Rental Income	$ 30,000	The total annual income generated from renting the property
Annual Operating Expenses	$ 10,000	The total annual costs for property taxes, insurance, etc.
Annual Net Profit	$ 20,000	The annual rental income minus the annual operating expenses
Annual Principal Reduction	$ 4,000	The portion of the mortgage payment that reduces the principal
Adjusted Profit	$ 24,000	The annual net profit plus the annual profit reduction
Return on Investment (ROI)	6.67%	The net profit divided by the total investment, expressed as percentage
Adjusted Return on Investment	8.00%	The adjusted net profit divided by the total investment, expressed as a percentage

Conclusion:

Utilizing a grid to analyze the performance of an investment property enables investors to systematically evaluate key financial metrics and make more informed decisions. By incorporating essential data such as rental income, operating expenses, net profit, and return on investment (ROI), a grid provides a clear and concise overview of the property's performance. This organized approach to investment analysis can help investors optimize their strategies for long-term success in the real estate market.

PHIL ZAIKOVATYY

As a rockstar in the real estate world, Phil has made a splash with over $100 million in sales volume, bringing his knowledge and mad skills to the industry. Rocking a BA in Finance/Real Estate and an MBA in Strategic Management, Phil's got the smarts to tackle those gnarly transactions and give strategic advice to all his clients.

Our main man Phil has got California Real Estate and Loan Originator licenses, and his experience stretches across all the rad aspects of real estate. He's been a listing agent, buyer's agent, handled rehab and construction projects, managed ADU build-outs and cost analysis, design, property management, and leasing. With 90% of his biz coming from repeat and referral clients, it's no surprise that Phil's commitment to excellence is off the charts.

But wait, there's more! Phil's got a keen eye for architecture, especially when it comes to Mid-Century Modern and ADU concepts. He brings a fresh perspective to his clients, and his achievements are anything but small potatoes. Phil's been featured in the LA Times, named a top 7 agent in the Studio City office of Dilbeck, and ranked as a top dog in Altera Realty. Plus, he's part of the elite Top Agent Network in LA County.

Phil's dedication to top-notch service knows no bounds. He's all about honesty, professionalism, integrity, and keeping an eye on the details. You can bet your bottom dollar that Phil's 100% committed to helping his clients reach their real estate dreams and blow their expectations out of the water.

In the exhilarating realm of real estate, Phil emerges as a true champion with a remarkable track record of over $100 million in sales volume. He brings a wealth of knowledge and expertise that empowers his clients to navigate the industry with confidence. Armed with a BA in Finance/Real Estate and an MBA in Strategic Management, Phil is equipped to expertly handle complex transactions and offer strategic insights to every client he serves.

Phil holds both California Real Estate and Loan Originator licenses, showcasing his versatility and mastery of various real estate sectors. Whether he's working as a listing agent, buyer's agent, rehab/construction overseer, ADU build-out and cost analysis manager, designer, property manager, or leasing specialist, Phil's commitment to excellence is unwavering. This dedication is evident in the fact that a staggering 90% of his business stems from repeat and referral clients—a true testament to his outstanding service.

Beyond his real estate prowess, Phil possesses a deep understanding of architecture, particularly in the areas of Mid-Century Modern and ADU concepts. This knowledge allows him to offer a unique and valuable perspective to his clients. His accomplishments in the industry are numerous, including being featured in the LA Times, recognized as a top 7 agent in the Studio City office of Dilbeck, and ranked as a leading agent in Altera Realty. Phil is also a member of the esteemed Top Agent Network in LA County.

Devoted to providing the highest caliber of service to his clients, Phil consistently demonstrates honesty, professionalism, integrity, and attention to detail. He remains steadfast in his commitment to help clients reach their real estate goals, always striving to exceed their expectations. As Zig Ziglar once said, "You can have everything in life you want if you will just help enough other people get what they want." Phil embodies this philosophy, ensuring his clients' success in their real estate journeys.

ANTHONY SEGIL

In the world of real estate, few names stand out as prominently as Anthony Segil. This maverick and visionary entrepreneur and property magnate, armed with a top-notch education, has amassed a staggering multi-million-dollar portfolio that boasts hundreds of doors and a legion of Accessory Dwelling Units (ADUs). A proud Trojan, Segil earned his undergraduate degree in Entrepreneurship from the University of Southern California (USC) and later returned to his beloved alma mater to bag an MBA, further honing his business acumen. As a pioneer in the Los Angeles real estate market, Segil has proven himself to be a thought leader and innovator, consistently staying ahead of the curve.

Anthony Segil's early involvement in the development of ADUs in Los Angeles demonstrates his forward-thinking approach and dedication to addressing the city's housing needs. When ADUs were still in their infancy, Segil recognized their potential to transform the local property landscape, creating affordable housing options while maximizing the value of existing properties. This foresight and willingness to embrace new ideas has solidified his reputation as a trailblazer in the industry.

Segil's multi-million-dollar portfolio is a testament to his strategic prowess and keen eye for lucrative investments. His impressive track record of acquiring and developing high-value properties, including residential and multifamily assets, showcases his ability to identify and capitalize on emerging market trends. With hundreds of doors under his belt, Segil has firmly established himself as a leading figure in the real estate sector.

As if all of this weren't enough, Anthony has been recognized by the City of Los Angeles for his civic and leadership contributions. He's not just a real estate mogul, dedicated to making his city a better place for everyone. His philanthropic efforts include supporting causes like education and safety, donning a cape of compassion and a mask of generosity, truly embodying the spirit of a modern-day superhero.

In summary, Anthony Segil is a real estate visionary whose multi-million dollar portfolio and pioneering work in the Los Angeles ADU market make him a true industry leader. His passion for innovation and commitment to sustainable development not only contribute to his personal success but also have a lasting impact on the communities in which he invests. As a thought leader, Segil's influence extends far beyond his own portfolio, inspiring the next generation of real estate professionals to think big and embrace change.

In the ever-evolving world of real estate, Anthony Segil is a beacon of light, guiding aspiring professionals towards success and inspiring those around him with his infectious enthusiasm and passion for his craft. As a multi-faceted entrepreneur, philanthropist, and author, he has left an indelible mark on the industry and the communities he serves.

So, if you're seeking a real estate guru who's got the brains, the humor, and the heart to guide you on your property journey, look no further than Anthony Segil. Join forces with this charismatic thought leader, innovator, and philanthropist, and together, you'll conquer the real estate world, one multi-million-dollar property at a time! And who knows? You might just end up with a 6 figure income, too. After all, with Anthony Segil as your mentor, the sky's the limit

www.ingramcontent.com/pod-product-compliance
Lightning Source LLC
Chambersburg PA
CBHW070919220526
45467CB00004B/1481